GREAT SMOKY MOUNTAINS COLORING BOOK

Written by Donna Cantrell
Illustrated by Oleksandra Kalynych

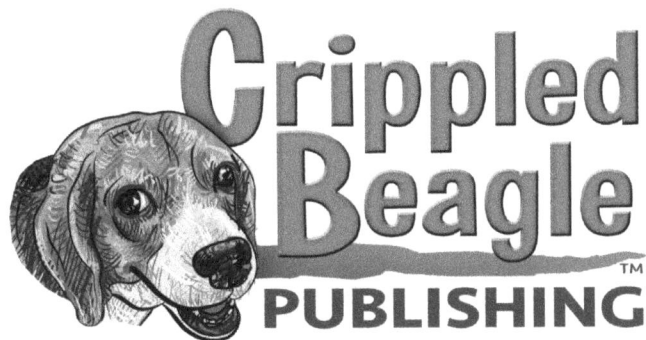

Crippled Beagle PUBLISHING ™

For discounts on group orders
contact Crippled Beagle Publishing.

dyer.cbpublishing@gmail.com
(865) 414-4017

"I will lift up my eyes to the hills—
From whence comes my help?
My help comes from the Lord,
Who made heaven and earth."
Psalm 121 NKJV

For many visitors the Primitive
Baptist Church invites thoughts of
old hymns and simpler times.

Huge hay rolls await winter storage
in a Cades Cove barn.

Brook trout and rainbow trout fill
the rushing waters of the
Great Smoky Mountains.

The starry night is a perfect backdrop for this mama red fox and her babies.

Trail horses are gentle and are trained to take riders on guided one-hour trips through the woods.

Mountain laurel clusters of pink
and white cover the riverbanks.

Bicyclists race away from a
wild boar, a destructive and
unwelcome inhabitant
of the Smokies.

Black bears are not harmless,
and visitors to the Park should
never go near bears.

WARNING

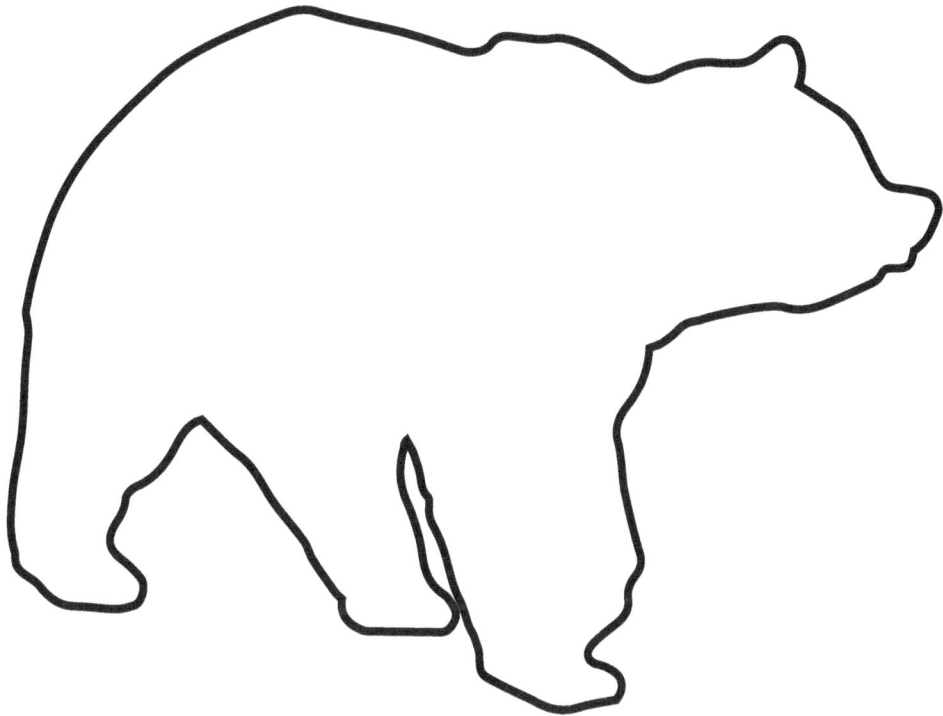

DO NOT
FEED
THE BEARS

This deep swimming hole,
below a cascading waterfall,
is called The Sinks.

Ready with sun protection, layered clothing, sturdy shoes, poles, food, and water, this young hiker sets off for a steep adventure on one of many trails in the Smoky Mountains.

A wise raccoon washes his breakfast of blackberries and beechnuts in a spring-fed creek at the edge of a field. Raccoons are often called "masked bandits."

Copperheads like rocks but can also be spotted in grassy areas and woodpiles. Hikers know to always step onto a log and not over it in case a copperhead is resting on the other side.

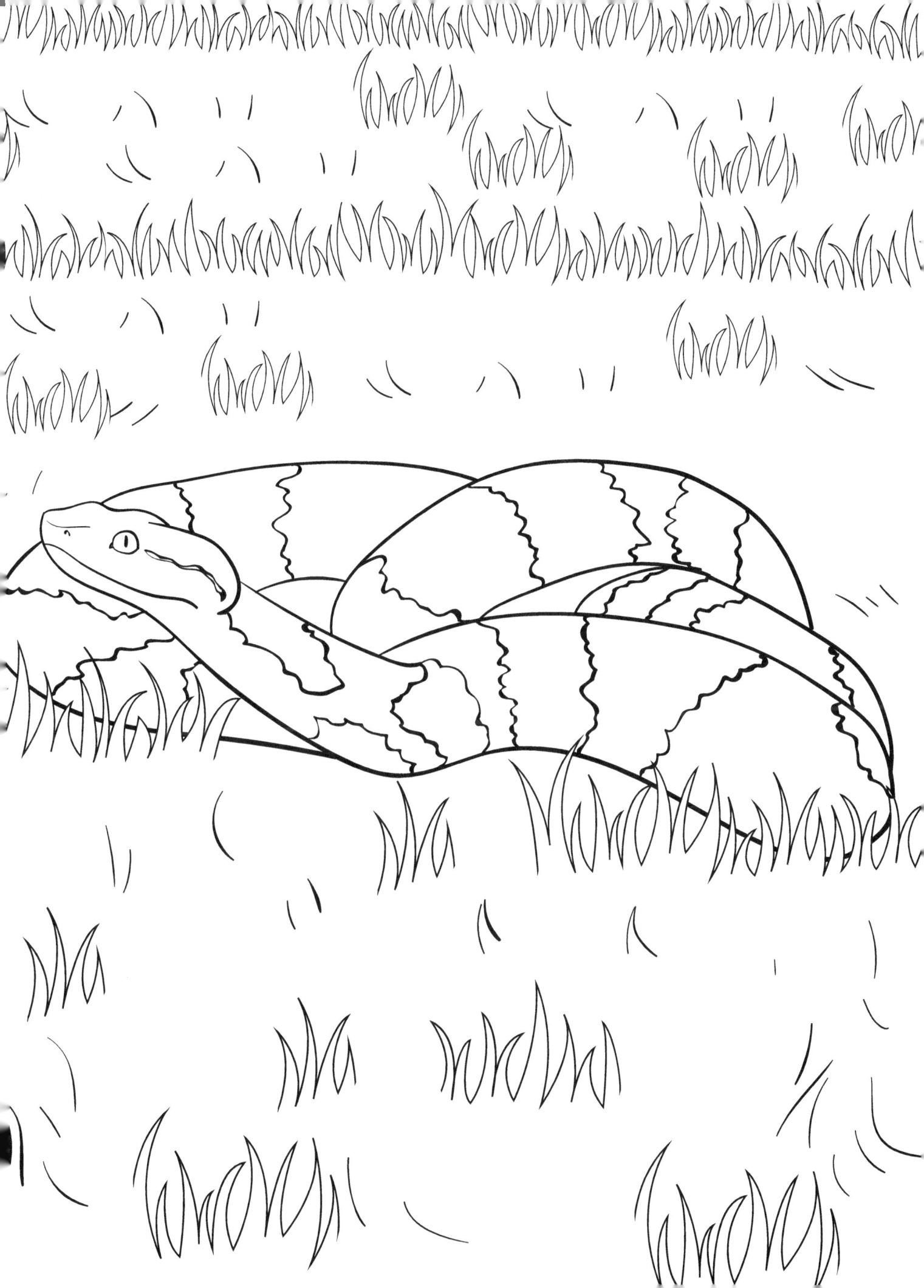

John Oliver Place is a popular attraction in Cades Cove. The Oliver family moved to the remote location deep in the Cove in the 1820s.

Wild orange day lilies freely decorate roadsides and fields of the Smoky Mountains.

Two boys and their grandmother relax at their Elkmont Campground site and plan the next day's adventures.

Turtles love to sunbathe on flat rocks in Little River.

Wild climbing roses weave through a wooden fence in front of a mountain farmstead.

Each June fireflies at Elkmont,
in the Smokies, fascinate young
and old with their synchronized
light shows.

Mountain water is extremely cold, crystal clear, and delightfully refreshing.

This colorful butterfly has plenty of room to spread its wings.

In a special place called Sunshine, Unincorporated—only six miles from one entrance to the Great Smoky Mountains National Park — river tubes await happy floaters who will soon cruise the currents of Little River.

Riverdance

This family enjoys a quiet lunch at one of the park's many picnic areas.

A stately bald eagle perches high in
a tree to overlook his domain.

A short wooden bridge enables hikers and visitors to experience the uninterrupted voice of the mountain stream.

A hornet nest hangs securely from a tree branch. A hornet nest has only one doorway and can be two feet long.

A vigilant park ranger
surveys the field inside
Cades Cove Loop.

A mama black bear and her cub
make their way across
a suspension bridge.

Children tell ghost stories while
warming themselves around
a cozy campfire.

An old oak tree is a perfect snack
bar and playground for
four happy squirrels.

Smoky Mountain elk sightings are rare and typically occur only in North Carolina's Cataloochee Valley.

The Great Smoky Mountains National Park covers 522,427 acres within Tennessee and North Carolina and is consistently the most visited national park in the National Park Service system.

NATIONAL
PAPK
SERVICE

Great Smoky
Mountains
National Park

White-blossomed trillium plants are among the more than 1500 varieties of wildflowers found in the Smokies. These ancient mountains have more flowering plants than any other national park in the United States.

This young woman dresses in authentic Cherokee attire. The Cherokee were the first native people to settle in the Smokies. Their culture is rich in history, impressive, and fascinating to study.

River otters are known for their playful water antics.

There are 150 trails in the Smokies. Many routes award hikers with breathtaking vistas and towering waterfalls. Trails vary in difficulty and elevation gain, but all trails are exciting passages through the majestic mountain landscape.

Brilliant red, orange, purple, and gold leaves create magnificent fall seasons, and millions of people flock to the mountains to see the change in colors.

S'mores are popular treats for campers. Graham crackers, roasted marshmallows, and chocolate bars make deliciously sweet desserts.

Beavers are free to build dams in their mountain stream homes.

Pioneer boys and girls were once educated in this one-room schoolhouse called Little Greenbrier School near Metcalf Bottoms.

In the summer multiple shades of green outline 2,900 miles of mountain springs, streams, creeks, and rivers.

This home on wheels lights the way to fun during a Smoky Mountain vacation.

On the outside this salamander looks like a lizard, but salamanders have soft, moist, brightly colored skin and no scales. Home to 30 species, the Smokies are the salamander capital of the world.

A farmer feeds sugar cane into a horse-powered mill to make sorghum molasses.

A cute chipmunk stops to eat a crunchy nut in the shade of mountain laurel.

Mt. LeConte hikers may spend the night in tiny wood cabins after their strenuous treks. LeConte Lodge, the highest lodging point in the Eastern United States, is accessible only by trail.

Ancient river rocks, huge boulders, and fast-moving water present exciting and challenging courses for kayak and canoe riders.

Sporting a short tail, a bobcat wanders through a grassy meadow.

This amazing barn is located in Oconaluftee Mountain Farm Museum just outside Cherokee, North Carolina.

**Black ants loom large
as picnic pests.**

Flat thin rocks are the best
for rock-skipping competitions on
the shallows of Little River.

Where to look for breakfast is
a big decision for this healthy
young rabbit.

A waterwheel generates power to a grinder that pounds corn into meal. This building is called a grist mill.

A four-mile climb through a huge old-growth forest, which houses some of the largest trees in the National Park, opens to a powerful waterfall called Ramsey Cascades.

Fly fishing, considered an art by many, is a popular endeavor in the magnificent streams of the Smokies. Fishermen especially like to snag the hard-to-catch rainbow trout.

A beautiful black and white skunk
rests on an old stump.
Armed with a stinky spray,
this skunk is confident.

Sugarlands Vistor Center is located
just outside Gatlinburg, Tennessee,
known as the Gateway
to the Smokies.

Minnows swim the cool clean
waters of the Smokies.
The Park contains 67 fish species.
Fatlips minnow and fathead
minnow are two funny
common names.

A little boy helps prepare a grilled hamburger supper for his family on the back porch of their mountain cabin.

Giant bullfrogs croak loudest
around sundown.

Breathtaking sunrises and sunsets at Clingmans Dome are two of the most colorful sights in the Smokies. With an elevation of 6,643 feet, Clingmans Dome is the highest point on the Appalachian Trail.

A spotted fawn sniffs out a tasty treat while two older deer remain alert for danger.

A homemade pioneer rag doll leans against a patchwork-quilted baby bed.

A wide-eyed owl keeps watch over the wildlife of his territory.

The Alum Cave Trail leads visitors though Arch Rock's slim tunnel, past Inspiration Point, and onward to the sandy soil under Alum Cave Trail's concave bluff, which is 80 feet tall and 500 feet long.

Hatchets, bows, and arrows can be examined in numerous exhibits in Smoky Mountain museums.

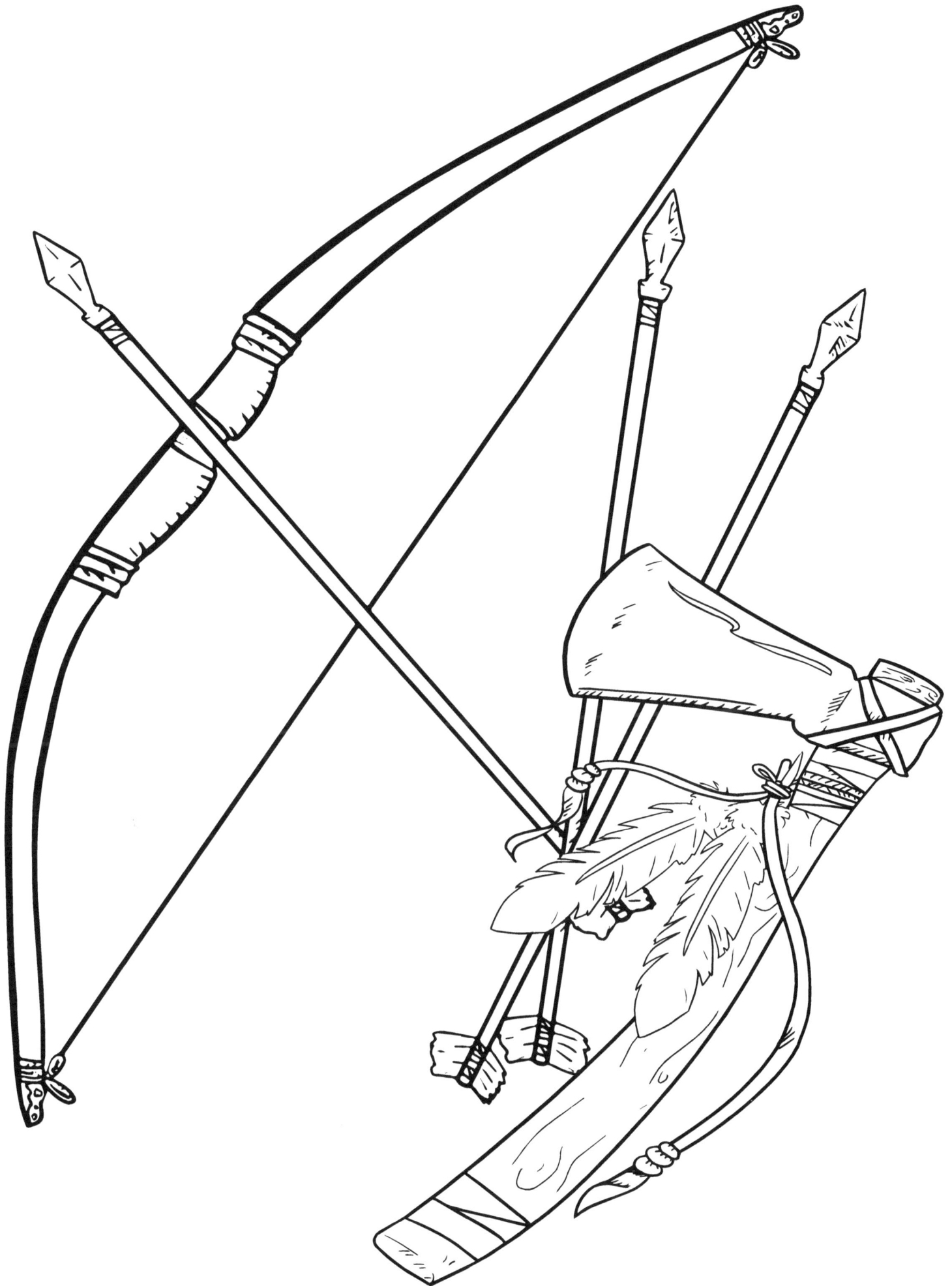

A great bald eagle checks
on her eggs.

Llamas carry supplies to LeConte Lodge by way of Trillium Gap Trail. At one point, the llama train walks behind Grotto Falls. At the top of the trip, trail guides reward the llamas with pancakes.

A teen angler carefully maneuvers a fuzzy dry fly into the path of a native brook trout.

An athletic boy gets ready to drop from high on a rope swing into Little River in Townsend, Tennessee.

PIM
POM

PRETTY PRESS

ISBN 978-1-965994-58-0

90000

9 781965 994580

www.ingramcontent.com/pod-product-compliance
Lightning Source LLC
Chambersburg PA
CBHW052113020426
42335CB00021B/2745